Introduc

Perhaps the finest area for walking in th National Park, the Dysynni Valley has att the years. These include Charles Darwin, tl painter Turner and travellers such as Franci .... Thomas Pennant to name just a few. Cadair Idris stands at the head of the valley, a proud and dramatic mountain with a fine south-west ridge going across Tyrrau Mawr. The woodlands are second to none with many rare and beautiful plants. Sessile oak trees, with their contorted trunks and branches, add a feeling of eccentricity to many of the walks. There are also some of the most beautiful waterfalls, rivers and streams in Wales.

Tywyn, at the seaward end, has attracted people for many years. In the 7th century St Cadfan founded a small religious community here when it was a well known staging post for pilgrims on their way to Bardsey Island. The church at Llanegryn houses a magnificent carved wood rood screen. Castell y Bere is perhaps the grandest historical site in the whole area, and has a superb view of the whole valley from its ramparts.

Whatever your level of fitness you will find, in these pages, walks to suit all abilities and tastes. **Walks 6, 7, 10** and **14** are the most demanding. Although an estimated time is given it depends on how many rests you have, as well as the speed of your walking. Such superb surroundings deserve the time to be enjoyed. All walks follow public rights of way and have been checked individually, but please be aware that things do change.

Each walk has a map and description which enables it to be followed without further help. However, on some of the more demanding excursions, it is advisable to take a map and compass and know how to use them. Take into account the weather (you can obtain an up-to-date forecast for this area on 09068 500414 [code 1403], charge) and dress accordingly. All of the walks cross sheep farming land at some stage so PLEASE keep your dog on a lead at ALL times whilst walking these routes.

Adhere to the country code. Enjoy the walks and have fun!

About the author, Des Marshall

Des has had a lifelong interest in mountaineering, climbing, walking, canyoning and caving. As well as being an advisor, trainer and assessor in outdoor activities, he has undertaken many expeditions worldwide but now focuses more on local excursions. After moving away a couple of years ago, the lure of the plethora of exciting walking and climbing became too much and he now lives in Cemmaes Road, near Machynlleth.

STEPPING THROUGH HISTORY

DESCRIPTION An almost totally level 2 mile walk in the very quiet and beautiful Dysynni Valley taking in Castell y Bere, Mary Jones' Chapel and Mary Jones' Cottage. There are some superb views and the walk is suitable for anyone of whatever age. Allow 2 hours to take in both a visit to the church and an exploration of Castell y Bere.

START Car park below Castell y Bere. There is also a picnic table and a bike security staple.

DIRECTIONS From Tywyn take the A493 towards Dolgellau. Go along this road until almost through the village of Bryncrug. Turn right in front of the church, signed Craig y Deryn, and left immediately after. This leads onto the minor road that goes up the Dysynni Valley and past Birds' Rock. Continue on this road until cross roads are met with a telephone box on your left. Here go straight ahead – signed Castell y Bere – to the car park below it.

I From the car park head towards Mary Jones' Chapel in the tiny hamlet of Llanfihangel-y-pennant. *A visit to this 12th century chapel is a must. Inside there is much of interest. Apart from the story of Mary Jones there is an amazing quilted 3D map of Bro Dysynni put together by 18 local people. Perhaps uniquely, there is a leper window. This is set into the wall at an angle so that those people with the disease could see the preacher in his pulpit as they were not allowed into the church. There are toilets (summer only) in the wood adjacent to the car park on the opposite side of the road.*

2 On leaving the chapel, turn left. Walk up the valley on the road. Ignore the left turn almost immediately and go straight ahead. *Looking back there is a great view of Birds' Rock.* Go past a stile on the right with a no parking sign. Continue past Tynyfach, a house and subsequent farm on the right and

go over either of the bridges spanning the Afon Cadair! *Just over the bridge there is an information board indicating Mary Jones' Cottage. Inside the ruin of her cottage stands a memorial to her.*

3 On the other side of the road there is waymark and a gate indicating Gernos. Go through this gate and follow the level track alongside the river. Go through a gate and another just as you reach Gernos. Keep left below the house *where there are also superb views of Birds' Rock.* Just beyond the house after a slight descent a ladder stile gives access to a flat green field which is crossed to another ladder stile with a much older stone stile immediately after, giving access onto a much rougher piece of land. Continue across this with the fence to your left until a concrete bridge is seen spanning the river. Go through the gate and cross the bridge to go through another gate. Two more gates through the farmyard of Maes-y-llan give access to a tarmac road.

4 Go down the road until clear of the farm buildings to a gate on the right with a waymark. Go through this gate and walk across the field close to the hedge on the left. Ignore the gate on the left and continue until a ladder stile can be crossed followed by a small concrete bridge into another field. Walk across this field with the hedge on your right until you meet a track. Follow this to the road. Cross the stile and turn left back to the car park at Castell y Bere.

This is now a good opportunity to explore the castle ruins. There is a shelter on the western side overlooking Birds' Rock. As with all other ruins please keep to the access paths and importantly do not walk or climb on the structures.

Castell y Bere is reputedly the last strong-hold of the Welsh against the English. It commands a fine strategic position. Llywelyn ap Iorwerth (Llywelyn the Great) started building the castle around 1221 having recovered control of Meirionnydd from his son Gryffydd. Although similar in design to other castles built by Llywelyn by having 'D' shaped towers north and south, a unique feature is the separation of the south tower from the rest of the castle by a ditch hewn out of the rock. Edward the First's Lieutenant besieged the castle during the war of 1282 – 83. When it fell on 25th April 1283 the English took it over leaving behind stone-masons and carpenters as part of a small garrison. During this period a walled yard was built linking the south tower to the rest of the castle. Edward intended keeping the castle as a centre of English power so started to build a town nearby. However, this did not flourish and the castle was retaken in 1294 by the Welsh during the revolt of Madog ap Llywelyn. It was retaken again by the English a year later but was subsequently destroyed and abandoned and there are no further records.

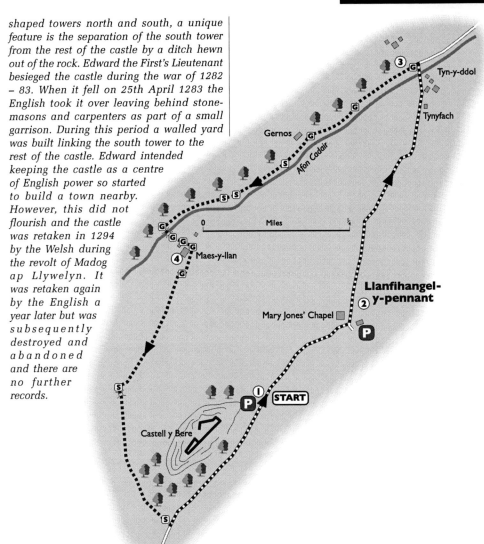

Mary Jones was born on the 16th December 1784 and moved to Ty'n y Ddol in Llanfihangel y Pennant very shortly after her birth, living most of her early life there. The church records show that she was baptised on the 19th December 1784. In 1800 Mary walked, barefoot, from her home, over the hills to Bala, a distance of 25 miles, where the Reverend Thomas Charles was distributing copies of the Welsh Bible. However, when Mary arrived he did not have a copy left to give her so he gave her his own copy having taken pity on her plight. It was said that this act gave birth to the formation of the British and Foreign Bible Society. Mary married a weaver from Bryncrug – Thomas Lewis – and lived at Tyn-y-winllan. She died in 1864 and was buried in the village chapel. Today many people, fascinated by her story, visit her grave in Bryncrug and the monument erected at her cottage in Llanfihangel y Pennant.

AFON DYSYNNI & AFON CADAIR CIRCULAR

DESCRIPTION This is a superb valley excursion, which can be divided into four separate walks. Great views, history and mainly easy walking. 8 miles but allow 5 hours to give time to look around Castell y Bere and Mary Jones' Chapel.

START At the layby close to Llanllwyda farm, camping and caravan site.

DIRECTIONS From Tywyn take the A493 towards Dolgellau. Go along this road until almost through the village of Bryncrug. Turn right in front of the church, signed Craig y Deryn, and left immediately after. This leads onto the minor road that goes up the Dysynni Valley and past Birds' Rock. Continue until a parking area is found on the right of the road just short of Llanllwyda farm. There is a picnic table and bicycle security staples.

I Although the first section is along a road it is quiet and has some good views. Go along the road past the turning into Llanllwyda farm, caravan and camping site. Keep walking along the road to a cross roads with a telephone box to your left. Go straight ahead – signed Castell y Bere – and walk past this and the car park there and on to Llanfihangel-y-pennant with Mary Jones' Chapel on your left. *(If you have not visited either of these it is well worth sparing the time to do so. See **Walk 1** for a brief notes on these).* There are toilets (summer only) adjacent to the car park on your right. Ignore the left turn immediately after the church and keep going straight on to Tyn-y-ddol. Cross the Afon Cadair by either of the bridges to an information board about Mary Jones and the remains of Mary Jones' cottage with a memorial to her.

2 On the opposite side of the road there is a waymark and a gate indicating Gernos. Go through this gate and follow the level track alongside the river. Go through a gate and another just as you reach Gernos. Keep left below the house *where there are also superb views of Birds' Rock.* Just beyond the house after a slight descent a ladder stile gives access to a flat green field which is crossed to another ladder stile with a much older stone stile immediately after, giving access onto a much rougher piece of land. Continue across this with the fence to your left until a concrete bridge is seen spanning the river. Instead of going over the river as in **Walk 1** keep going along the rough path to a stile. Go over this to a smoother continuation of the path. Continue across two more stiles to eventually reach some farm buildings. Cross over the stile ahead here. Turn left and follow a short section of path cum streambed to another stile. Go over this to reach a tarmac road by a disused chapel between Bodilan Fach and Pen-y-meini.

3 Turn right and walk up the road to a stile on your left. Go over this and walk quite steeply up the hill with the fence to your right to a track. Turn right and continue up the track between fences to a stile among holly bushes. Go over this to join a track. Cross over this and follow waymark posts bearing left down through a larch coppice and over the ladder stile and on to another marker post. Continue to another ladder stile and walk through a gap in the fence ahead and, keeping the pond down to your left, descend slightly to a footbridge and a stile at the edge of the wood. Cross over these and keep to the right edge of the field below the trees and continue to a marker post by the ruins of Dol-y-maen. At the post turn left to cross the field to a gate where you turn right to follow the drainage ditch on your right and fence on your left to a ladder stile. Go over this and very shortly after to your right by a gate a stile is crossed. Follow the track with the fence to your left and on through a gate. Pass this and continue through a grove of alder and oak trees into the open field by a fence corner on your left. Bear slightly to your right, to a short length of wall and a gate to the right of it.

4 Go through the gate and keep the fence to your left and on to another gate. After passing through this a farm track is reached.

through trees to some farm buildings where there is a waymark. Go straight ahead through the buildings and down to a

(map with labels: Tyn-y-ddol, Tynyfach, Gernos, Afon Cadair, Maes-y-llan, Llanfihangel-y-pennant, Bodilan Fach, Pen-y-meini, Mary Jones' Chapel, Castell y Bere, Dol-y-maen, Dysefin-uchaf, Pont Ystumanner, Afon Dysynni, ysefin Farm, Llanllwyda, START, 0 Miles ¼)

prominent farm track. Turn left down this track with tarmac strips to a junction. Just before this there is a waymark on a tree on your left. Bear left at the junction keeping the house with a fine, but old, circular gazebo to your right. Keep on this track to join a narrow tarmac road. Turn right and after passing through an ornamental gateway turn left for a short distance to cross over the Afon Dysynni. Immediately beyond the bridge there is a stile leading onto the river embankment.

(Great view of Birds' Rock from here). Turn left along this. Keep right of some farm buildings at Dysefin-uchaf and continue through a gate and keep the farm buildings to your left. Keep going along the track to a gate before Dysefin Farm. Go through this into the farmyard and another by the farmhouse. A short distance further you join a narrow tarmac road.

5 Turn right along this and continue until you reach a cattle grid. Cross over this to a waymark just beyond. Go right here through a gate and follow the track across the field to a gate by a very fine oak tree. Continue through the gate and walk up hill for a short distance to a ladder stile left of a gate. Go over this and cross the field to another ladder stile which is climbed over to follow the fence on your left. Continue to a waymark and ignore the old gate to its left to keep on the same line following the fence. At the field corner go through a black metal gate to go slightly downhill a short distance

6 Follow the embankment. This is presumably man-made to prevent the fields being engulfed when the Afon Dysynni floods. Birds' Rock looms on the right. *Cormorants nest on the crag which at one time – not that long ago – was by the sea! They still catch fish – from the crystal clear waters of the river.* Keep following the embankment. Go over a ladder stile close to where the road passes and continue to a stile opposite Wern Farm on the road side. Cross another ladder stile before reaching the end of the embankment. Turn right before the gate leading into the caravan and camping site to follow the fence on your left to a ladder stile. Climb over this to the tarmac road which is followed back through the farm to the road. Turn right back to your car.

BASTION OF THE VALLEY

DESCRIPTION This is a superb walk up the most prominent and striking feature in the Dysynni Valley – Craig yr Aderyn or Birds' Rock. Here is the only inland nesting ground for Cormorants in Europe and, possibly, the world! Other birds use this as their nesting ground, kestrels, ravens and the rare chough. There are also concentric Bronze and Iron-Age fortifications on the lower summit. Although steep at the start the effort is amply rewarded by increasingly spectacular views as height is gained along the whole length of the valley from the coast to the summit of Cadair Idris. This is followed, in complete contrast, by a level stroll along the bank of the beautiful Afon Dysynni. 5 miles but allow 3 hours.

START At the layby close to Llanllwyda farm, camping and caravan site.

DIRECTIONS From Tywyn take the A493 towards Dolgellau. Go along this road until almost through the village of Bryncrug. Turn right in front of the church, signed Craig y Deryn, and left immediately after. This leads onto the minor road that goes up the Dysynni Valley and past Birds' Rock. Continue until a parking area is found on the right of the road just short of Llanlwyda farm. There is a picnic table and bicycle security staples.

I Climb over the stile next to the waymark post and follow the path to join a larger track. Turn left up this and go steadily uphill to where the track rises more gently. *There are great views up the Pennant Valley towards Cadair Idris.* Where the wall on the left ends a fence starts. From this point go right and ascend on a vague path up the grassy slope. The path becomes much more defined as it passes through some tiny rock outcrops. *The lower of the Birds' Rock summits can be seen straight ahead.* Continue on this grassy way bearing slightly left. *Just before the path becomes steeper there is a seat on which to sit down and admire the*

view. From the seat after your rest continue up the steeper part which is now quite wide to the crest where the path splits. Bear right and pass to the right of a pile of stones on a faint but wide path up to the left hand end of the lower fort boundary. A path goes to the right between the lower and upper fort to a cairn. Another cairn a short distance away on the well marked path is passed. Continue past the TV aerial on your right and up to the 'popular' summit of Birds' Rock. *Unrivalled views of the whole length of the valley from Cadair Idris all the way to the sea.*

2 From here a prominent, quartz speckled, broken cliff is seen below the highest summit and a well marked, but narrow, path some 200 metres to the left of a 10m high band of grey rock a little lower. Head across to this path and follow it up to a fence to where it turns 90 degrees to the left. Keep following the fence until you can bear right through an area of quartz stones and on to the crest. Turn right along the narrow path to reach the substantial summit cairn doubling as a shelter. *More spectacular views are to be had from here.*

3 Over to the left, when looking out to sea, a prominent cairn can be seen on the next, but lower summit, point 231. Although there is no path it is easily attained by descending to the col followed by an easy ascent to the cairn on top and a few metres further on, another. From this cairn head over to the very substantial wall on your left. Follow this steeply down, bypassing a rather large gorse bush on the right, to reach a tarmac road at Bwlch y Maen.

4 Go down the road through a gate. Continue along the road slightly up and then down past a hairpin bend to a gate. Do not go through the gate but follow the direction of the waymark, continue down with the fence to your left to a stile. Over this and follow the fenced off path to a stile which is crossed and keeping the fence to your left walk on to another stile. Over this and, IMPORTANTLY, go a few paces forwards then turn left down the slope to the driveway of Erw Wadd. Turn left a few paces to

a waymark. (Follow the home-made signs). From here go down the grassy slope to the driveway. Go right along the driveway to an acute turning left and go straight ahead past a ruin and gradually ascend. Keep going ahead. When the path levels out there is a stile with a public footpath sign to the right. Go over the stile and head slightly right across the field to another stile. Over this and into the wood. An indistinct path leads down through this wood to a stile and a little further another leads on to the road.

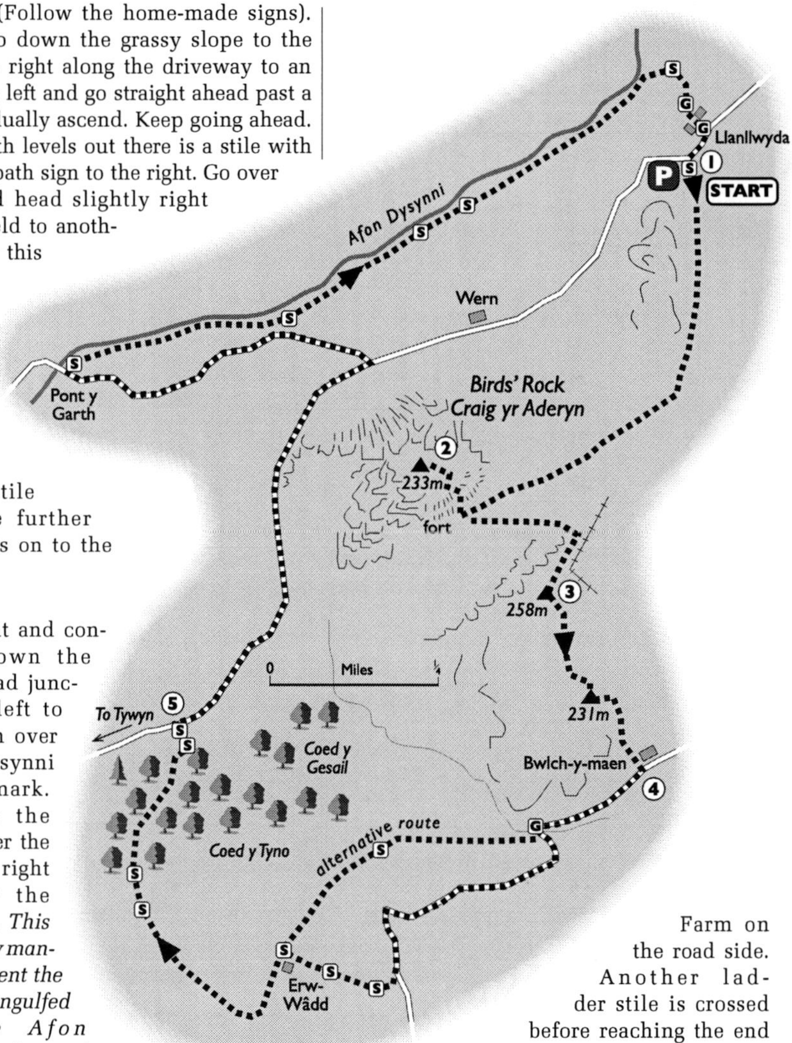

5 Turn right and continue down the road to a road junction. Turn left to Pont y Garth over the Afon Dysynni and a waymark. Just before the bridge go over the stile on the right and follow the embankment. *This is presumably man-made to prevent the fields being engulfed when the Afon Dysynni floods. Birds' Rock looms on the right. Cormorants nest on the crag which at one time – not that long ago – was by the sea! They still catch fish – from the crystal clear waters of the river.* Keep following the embankment. Go over a ladder stile close to where the road passes and continue to a stile opposite Wern

Farm on the road side. Another ladder stile is crossed before reaching the end of the embankment. Turn right before the gate leading into the caravan and camping site to follow the fence on your left to a ladder stile. Climb over this to the tarmac road which is followed back through the farm to the road. Turn right back to your car.

Map labels: Llanllwyda, START, Wern, Birds' Rock, Craig yr Aderyn, Afon Dysynni, Pont y Garth, 233m, fort, 258m, 231m, Bwlch-y-maen, To Tywyn, Coed y Gesail, Coed y Tyno, alternative route, Erw-Wâdd, Miles

AROUND FOEL CAE'RBERLLAN

DESCRIPTION This is a fine and very diverse walk. – an old castle, an ancient church, waterfalls and a wild stretch of upland. 5 miles, 3 hours.

START The Post Office/Community Centre/ Café car park in the middle of Abergynolwyn.

DIRECTIONS From Tywyn take the A493 Dolgellau road as far as Bryncrug. Turn right here on to the B4405 signed Talyllyn. At Abergynolwyn turn right opposite the Railway Inn into the car park.

1 Go down the road right of the Railway Inn and signed to Castell y Bere. Go over the Dysynni and note the footpath on the right by the river for your return. Continue very steeply up to a road junction. Turn left here to walk down then up a small rise. At the top of this is a stile on your right with a marker, signed Llwybr Cyhoeddus.

2 Cross the stile and continue along the obvious path half-left. Several waymark poles indicate the way. Go over a slabby rock that looks as though it was man-made to a green track. Cross over this to a marker pole hidden under oak and hawthorn trees. Continue horizontally to a stile over a fence. Cross this and down steps. A short section of path leads to wall corner. Turn left keeping the wall to your left to where a waymark diverts you away from the wall slightly. A green track is met and is followed to a gate. Go through this, then go immediately left and then right to go over a stile. Follow the green path down – good view of Castell y Bere from here. The path meets a good track which is followed to the right until a green kissing gate is found on the left. Go through this and go half-right across the field to join the minor road at a stile.

3 Turn right and walk along the road. Go past the car park for Castell y Bere. If you have not visited the ruin before then this is a good time to do so. (See walk 1 for brief information about the history). Continue down the hill from here towards Llanfihangel-y-pennant and Mary Jones' Chapel. A visit here is recommended if you have not already done so. (See walk 1 for brief historical notes about Mary Jones).

4 Opposite the church gate and to the right of the car park – toilets to the right in the wood (summer only) – a waymarked track goes past a house on the right and reaches a stile. Go over this to walk up the well marked path with a lovely stream on your right with several small waterfalls. A stile will be seen ahead as the path levels. Go over this and continue uphill to where the path levels once more. Keep going with the stream to your right and ignore the prominent stile on your right. By what appears to be a split rock go up to your left to join a track and turn right along it to a ladder stile by two gates. Cross this and follow track that becomes a path. The ruins of Nant-yr-eira can be seen in the distance. Go over two small streams and pass Nant-yr-eira to the right and continue to a stile.

5 Go over the ladder stile and continue, gently rising over a short rocky section to where a low wall is passed on your right. From here go half-right to join a track and to what appears to be a ruin but is in fact sheep pens. To the right of the pens is a ladder stile. Go over this to join the good track. This is followed downhill to where a waymark indicates a sharp turn right off the track. Go down this narrow path – steep in parts – round a hairpin bend to a stile. Bear left over this to a ladder stile. Cross this and descend the field to the left hand corner to another ladder stile leading onto a minor road. Turn right along the minor road. Continue along the road almost to Abergynolwyn to a waymark indicating a left turn. Go down the steps away from the road to a stile. Continue down more well-spaced steps and follow the well-trodden path over three more stiles before walking down to the river. Follow the stone slabs by the river to a kissing gate on the right of the bridge. Go through this gate and turn left down the road back to your car in the village.

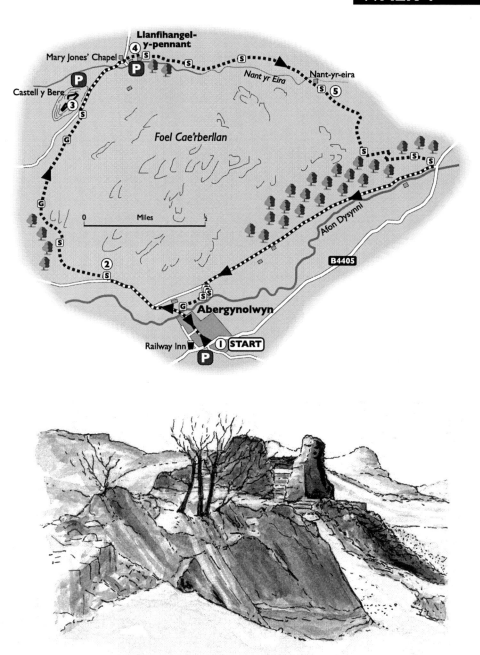

Castell y Bere, with Birds' Rock in the distance

AFON DYSYNNI & AROUND MYNEDD RHIWERFA

DESCRIPTION A good walk taking the narrow confines of the infant Afon Dysynni as it tumbles down from Abergynolwyn into the Pennant Valley. This is followed by lovely rural walking around the hill – back to Abergynolwyn. 4½ miles, 2½ hours.

START The Post Office/Community Centre/Café car park in the middle of Abergynolwyn.

DIRECTIONS From Tywyn take the A493 Dolgellau road as far as Bryncrug. Turn right here on to the B4405 signed Talyllyn. At Abergynolwyn turn right opposite the Railway Inn into the car park.

1 From the car park join the road and turn left to walk past the Railway Inn on your right and past a play area. Turn right immediately beyond this and walk down the street to a footbridge on your left over the stream. Go through the gate at the end of the bridge and follow the path which passes a house to your left. Go up a few steps to follow a short length of paved path to a gate. Go through this and continue along a well marked but narrow path – take care here as there are steep drops at the start) high above the clear waters of the Afon Dysynni. Pass Cow Rock and continue to a gate. Go through this to follow a mainly level path to another gate. Carry on through this and on to a black/white marker post. Go up left here to avoid a landslip to the top of a small rise and a track junction. Drop down the right hand track to join the river which is followed on its left bank to pass a gate on the right at a long-since-broken fence. Continue to another gate at a house – Rhiwlas – on the left.

2 Go past this and in a few metres go over a stile on your left. Climb up a steep field trending slightly left to go over a stile in a clump of trees at the left hand corner. Continue up the hill via a wide grassy depression passing a large gorse clump to the left. Bear right slightly to end up at a small col between a high left-hand rocky knoll and a lower right-hand one. Go across the field more or less straight ahead to a gate and stile on the left of it. *There are good views of Birds' Rock here.* Once over the stile turn left to follow the fence keeping it to your left. A well worn path develops as a gate is approached. Go through this and, just the other side of the stream go half-left to a stile. Cross this and climb up steeply to the right to the marker post seen from below. From here walk across to a stile and go over it. Follow a raised section across the field to a gate. Go through this onto a track – Gelli ddraenen is down to your right.

3 Go left up the track to a tarmac road and turn left again through a wood gate and walk along the road to Rhiwerfa. Continue past here and follow the very steep track down to the B4405 ignoring the forestry road on your left. Cross over the road, turn left and return to the start in Abergynolwyn along a wide, grassy verge.

The distinctive features of Cow Rock are the very sturdy iron rings fixed into the rock along with carved troughs. The farmer used these rings to tether his cows when he wanted to feed or milk them without the hassle of driving them to his farm!

A whirlpool once existed at confluence of the Nantgwernol and Afon Dysynni, hence the name Abergynolwyn – aber means mouth of the river and gwyn olwyn means white wheel or whirlpool.

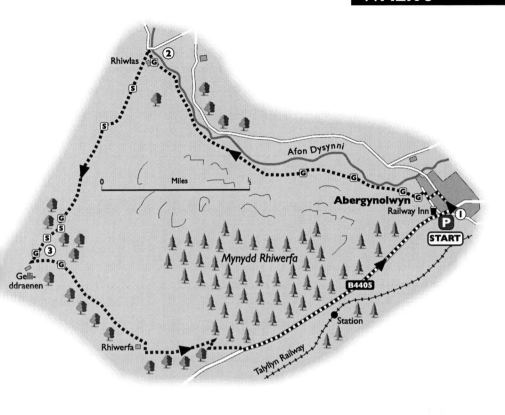

Fancy a pint?

TYRRAU MAWR & CRAIG Y LLYN CIRCULAR

DESCRIPTION A grand mountain excursion. The track as far as point numbered *560* is of great antiquity as it was the most direct way for people to get to Dolgellau, their local market town and seat of the Quarter Sessions. There are superb views along the ridge from point *560* to Craig-y-llyn, especially down towards the Cregennan Lakes, Mawddach Estuary and Barmouth. Care is required towards the end of the walk from the col just before point *501* for a short distance to pick the right line to the ruins at Craig Maes-y-llan. 6 – 7 hours.

START The car park on the opposite side of the road from Mary Jones' Chapel in Llanfihangel-y-pennant. There are toilets (summer only) in the wood adjacent.

DIRECTIONS From Tywyn take the A493 towards Dolgellau. Go along this road until almost through the village of Bryncrug. Turn right, in front of the church, signed Craig y Deryn and left immediately after leads onto the minor road that goes up the Dysynni Valley and past Birds' Rock. Continue on this road until cross roads are met with a telephone box on the left. Here go straight ahead – signed Castell y Bere. Continue past the car park there and go downhill to the car park in Llanfihangel-y-pennant.

I From the car park turn right onto the road and walk up the valley to the bridges spanning the Afon Cadair. Cross this then turn right, past the site of Mary Jones' Cottage. Go through a gate and continue up the tarmac road until it ends at Gwastadfryn.

2 Go through the gate and walk up the gravel track, through a larch wood and a gate. Continue steadily uphill on the well-marked track going through two gates and over four stiles to reach Hafodty Gwastadfryn. Bear right here and go over the waymarked stile. Cross the bridge over the stream. Walk up

a rougher track to a junction. Go right up the hill on the grassy track to a ladder stile on the right. Follow the waymarks and the grassy track which bears sharp right at a wooden post and continues as a rutted path. It levels out and a ladder stile and a gate are seen ahead. Go over the stile and continue along the level path which soon rises gradually to the col at 560m.

3 Turn left and follow the gradually ascending path alongside the fence on your right. Pass a huge pile of stones, complete with shelter on your left, to the summit of Tyrrau Mawr, 660m. Go over the summit stile and follow the path along the ridge, still with the fence on your right. A gradual descent leads to a point where a ladder stile on your right can be crossed for superb views of the Cregennan Lakes far below. Continue along the ridge ignoring the many ladder stiles on your right. Ahead are Craig-y-Llyn and Llyn Cyri. A steep descent leads to a col. Go over the ladder stile here and follow the fence. Walk over the next rise and descend to a col. A steep ascent leads to the summit of Craig-y-llyn 622m.

4 Descend gradually to Twll yr Ogof and go over the ladder stile to your right where a steep descent leads to a col. From the col follow the fence down to your left to reach a track with a gate on your right. From the gate go left 50m along the track. Turn right. CARE is needed here to pick the right line downhill on a vague grassy path. Keep above, and well to the left of, the narrowing and steepening stream on you right until level with a ruined wall where a much better path reveals itself and leads to some obvious ruins – Craig Maes-y-llan. There is a ladder stile to the right of the ruins.

5 Climb over the stile and go half right to a wooden pole. Go down the rough track, over the next stile and down the grassy track until a fence can be followed down to a gate on the right. Go through this to a ruin which has a ladder stile next to it. Cross this and descend the field passsing isolated boulders and a solitary hawthorn to climb over another ladder stile. Walk half-right and go through the lower of two gates. Continue along the track to a farmyard which is crossed via two gates. After the second gate bear left keeping Nant Caw-fawr farmhouse on your right to a gate, and a very short distance further another with a waymark. Go through this and turn immediately left along a rough track (DO NOT go down the road) that rises slightly, then levels before some farm buildings. Pass these on the right to a stile over the wall on your right. Follow the fence alongside a stream to your right. Keep following the fence downhill to the next gate.

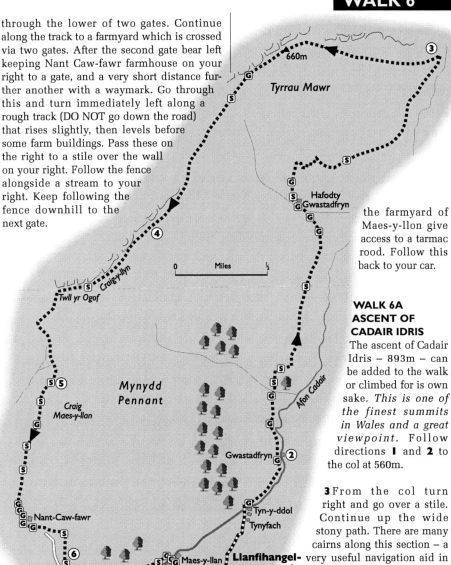

the farmyard of Maes-y-llon give access to a tarmac rood. Follow this back to your car.

WALK 6A
ASCENT OF
CADAIR IDRIS

The ascent of Cadair Idris – 893m – can be added to the walk or climbed for is own sake. *This is one of the finest summits in Wales and a great viewpoint.* Follow directions **1** and **2** to the col at 560m.

3 From the col turn right and go over a stile. Continue up the wide stony path. There are many cairns along this section – a very useful navigation aid in mist for which the mountain is notorious. As you get close to the summit the path becomes steeper, rockier and is very close to the cliff edge at one point. The rocks underfoot are particularly slippery when wet. Allow 1½ hours for the 3 mile round trip from the col (point **3**) OR 6 hours for the 10½ mile walk from the valley if you are only climbing Cadair Idris.

6 DO NOT go through this. Turn left along a green path and go over a stile. Keep the wall to your right and continue along, going over three more stiles to the concrete bridge over the Afon Cadair. A gate gives access to the bridge. Cross this and go through another gate. Two more gates leading through

THE DEVIL'S VALLEY

DESCRIPTION A good walk that starts in the upper reaches of the Dysynni Valley and after a climb goes along a wild upland valley before dropping almost to Talyllyn before climbing up again to the Nant yr Eira Valley. 7½ miles, allow 4½ hours.

START The car park on the opposite side of the road from Mary Jones' Chapel in Llanfihangel-y-pennant. There are toilets (*summer only*) in the wood adjacent.

DIRECTIONS From Tywyn take the A493 towards Dolgellau. Go along this road until almost through the village of Bryncrug. Turn right, in front of the church, signed Craig y Deryn and left immediately after leads onto the minor road that goes up the Dysynni Valley and past Birds' Rock. Continue on this road until cross roads are met with a telephone box on the left. Here go straight ahead – signed Castell y Bere. Continue past the car park there and go downhill to the car park in Llanfihangel-y-pennant.

I Turn right after leaving the car park and walk up the valley to a stile on your right by a 'no parking' sign. Go over the stile and continue up the prominent track to another stile (*requested May 2007*). Continue to a gate and go through this to keep on the track passing a waymark on your left. Keep going uphill to where the track levels out. Bear left to a ladder stile to the right of a gate. (Ignore the two gates and stile on your right). Go over the ladder stile and continue past a larch plantation on your left. Cross over the stream (*fun in wet weather!*) at the end of the plantation. Continue along the track – *good views down the valley to Birds' Rock* – to a gate just beyond a bridge over the stream.

2 Go through the gate and continue uphill for 100m to a path on your right. Follow this grassy zig-zag path uphill. As height is gained a ruin is seen on the skyline. Head towards this. From the ruin a gap in the wall

is seen ahead. Go through this gap passing between two prominent boulders (*the right hand one has prominent quartz streaks*) and go half-left up to a ladder stile to the left of a gate. Pencoed is on your left. Go over a sleeper footbridge to go over another ladder stile almost immediately. *Superb views down the valley to Birds' Rock and the sea from here.* Go half-right across the field to cross another ladder stile over a wall. Follow the wall on your right until you reach a gate with a stile to the left. Go over the stile and follow a faint path half-left going slightly downhill to reach a better path at a small stream. Cross over this and cross a damp section to a drier continuation. Keep following the track with boggy sections to some ruins. Pass just above these and continue along a well-marked track again with boggy bits and a stream. Along this section there is a large flat stone among some rocks, although it is extremely difficult to locate as the surrounding vegetation has grown over most of it. This is 'The Devil's Rock'. Pass below a ruin seen up to your left and keep going in the same line. After a short uphill section another much more pronounced track is followed to the right along a level stretch to a ladder stile to the right of a gate.

3 Go over the ladder stile and follow the continuation of the track to another ladder stile. Go over this to yet another which is just below a ruin with a TV aerial! Keep on the track and descend to a ladder stile just before Rhiwogof farm. Go over this stile and cross the track. Pass below some sheep pens to another ladder stile left of a gate. Cross this and rejoin the main farm track beyond the buildings. Walk downhill, over a cattle grid (turning left here and walking steeply down to reach Pen-y-bont Hotel on the shore of Tal-y-llyn) and follow the rough

Tyn-y-ddôl

Tynyfach

Llanfihangel-y-pennant

Mary Jones' Chapel

START

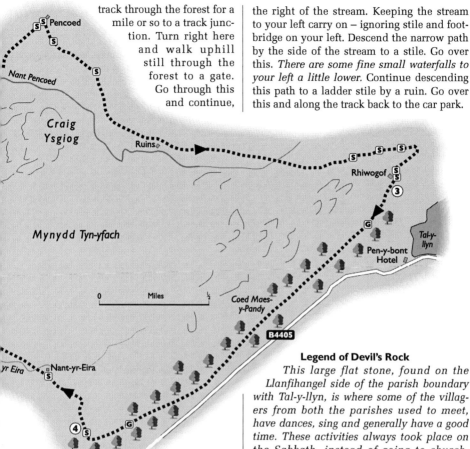

track through the forest for a mile or so to a track junction. Turn right here and walk uphill still through the forest to a gate. Go through this and continue, still uphill. Pass the waymark on walk 7 to a ladder stile where the track has levelled off. Go over the stile – with sheep pens to your right.

4 Follow the track a short distance before following the wall line on your left until it ends. Continue a short distance to find a good track which is followed down to a ladder stile just before the ruin of Nant-y-Eira. Go over the stile and follow the grassy track gently down to cross the Nant-y-Eira stream and pass below another ruin. Continue across the field to where the track becomes more pronounced and keep going to a ladder stile. Go over this. 100m further on bear left of the track down a grassy area to a path to the right of the stream. Keeping the stream to your left carry on – ignoring stile and footbridge on your left. Descend the narrow path by the side of the stream to a stile. Go over this. *There are some fine small waterfalls to your left a little lower.* Continue descending this path to a ladder stile by a ruin. Go over this and along the track back to the car park.

Legend of Devil's Rock

This large flat stone, found on the Llanfihangel side of the parish boundary with Tal-y-llyn, is where some of the villagers from both the parishes used to meet, have dances, sing and generally have a good time. These activities always took place on the Sabbath, instead of going to church. However, on one Easter Sunday when the parishioners were half way through their festivities the Devil appeared in their midst, dressed as an ass! He let out a terrible howl that made even the mountain tremble. Fear and dread filled the assembled throng. They fled in absolute terror back to their respective churches and prayed for forgiveness. It was many years before anyone dared to venture back to that spot until two shepherds were appointed to the area, one from Pencoed and the other from Rhiwogof. Approaching the rock with trepidation they discovered the hoof-prints embedded into the rock. Since then other shepherds have carved their initials into the rock. Apparently, the oldest inscription is 1564.

A GLIMPSE OF THE DYSYNNI VALLEY

DESCRIPTION A walk through farmland using, in part, a very quiet minor road and passing through a wood of fine, contorted sessile oak trees towards the end. Some good views of the upper Dysynni Valley and Cadair Idris. 3½ miles, 2½ hours.

START The Car Park for Dolgoch Falls on the B4405. There is a parking charge (£1 for 4 hours or £2 all day, May 2007).

DIRECTIONS From Tywyn take the A493 Dolgellau road as far as Bryncrug. Turn right here on to the B4405 signed Talyllyn. The prominent car park close to the Dolgoch Hotel is seen on your right before reaching Abergynolwyn.

I From the car park go right back on to the B4405 and turn left back towards Tywyn a short distance to the left hand bend. On the right there is a waymark and stile. Go up a few steps, go over the stile and turn left. At a waymark go half-right up the field to a yellow marker post by the fence on the left. Follow the fence up to the corner and go straight ahead below a large oak tree on your right (white arrow) and on up to a stile. Go over this to a yellow marker post ahead. From this go slightly right to a waymark and stile with a public footpath sign. Continue with the fence to your left to a ladder stile. Cross this and a footbridge immediately beyond and walk ahead up to a yellow marker post. Bear left to a waymark and stile to join a minor road.

2 Turn right up the road and go through the houses and go round a 90 degree bend in the road and on through a gate. Continue up the road, round a hairpin bend up to and through a gate. Keep following the tarmac road around another hairpin bend and descend. Pass through another gate and continue along the road to Bwlch-y-maen. Go through the gate just before the house and keep on the road to go round a right hand bend to a gate. Go through this and continue with great views of the Dysynni Valley and Cadair Idris ahead. Keep going and on through a wooden gate to Rhiwerfa.

3 Go past the house and start to descend. After a few metres a waymark is seen on your right. Turn right here and go down a steep but wide path through a wonderful wood of contorted sessile oak trees to a gate. Pass through this and continue down to go through another to follow the path above the farm buildings of Tan-y-coed-uchaf. At a track junction bear right to a gate with waymark. Go through the gate and follow path ahead with a fence on your left. Continue to a stile. Cross this and on to a gate just before Tan-y-coed-isaf. Go through the gate and turn right to take the waymarked path that goes behind the house. Continue to a gate. Go through this and on to climb over a ladder stile. Keep going along the path to reach a gate. Go through this, passing another gate and on to a stile – the one you climbed over at the start. Cross over this to join the B4405 to retrace your steps back to your car at Dolgoch.

16

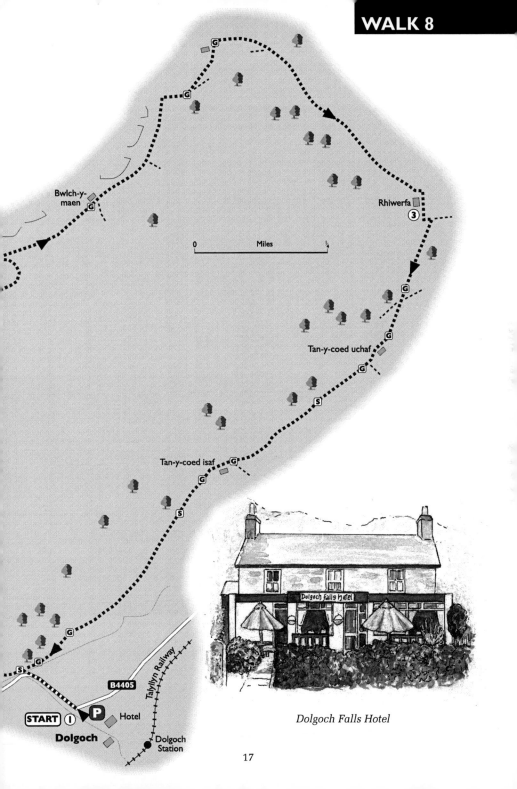

Bwlch-y-maen

Rhiwerfa

3

0 Miles

Tan-y-coed uchaf

Tan-y-coed isaf

Dolgoch Falls Hotel

Tabyllyn Railway

B4405

START **①** **P** Hotel

Dolgoch

Dolgoch Station

DOLGOCH FALLS

DESCRIPTION A lovely, though quite popular, walk especially in summer which can be very enthralling when the waterfalls are in spate after a period of heavy rainfall. The steeper sections of the path, particularly the steps, can be quite slippery when wet. DO NOT ENTER ANY OF THE ADITS THAT YOU PASS DURING THE WALK. 1½ miles, but allow an hour to admire the falls or it can take all day if having a picnic! There are four bridges each having a poem attached to them. These poems were written by children from the Primary School at Bryncrug.

START The Car Park for Dolgoch Falls on the B4405. There is a parking charge (£1 for 4 hours or £2 all day, May 2007).

DIRECTIONS From Tywyn take the A493 Dolgellau road as far as Bryncrug. Turn right here on to the B4405 signed Talyllyn. The prominent car park close to the Dolgoch Hotel is seen on your right before reaching Abergynolwyn.

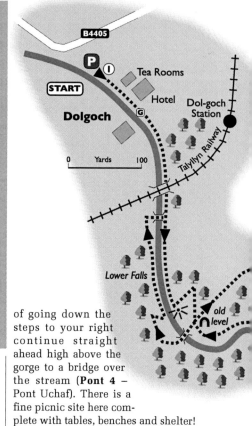

1 From the car park go up the narrow tarmac road passing to the right of the Dolgoch Falls Hotel. Go through the substantial metal gate ahead and keep following the tarmac track ignoring the sign to Dolgoch Station on your left. Keeping the stream on your right go under the railway bridge and ignore the footbridge on your right. Continue slightly uphill to the viewing area for the lower falls. There is an adit here that leads into the base of a shaft. Return a few metres to the information board and go steeply up steps ignoring the track that continues beyond the metal gate to Dolgoch Station. Keep on this rough track to a junction. Go right to overlook the falls. There is a fenced-off deep shaft to your left. Just before the foot bridge turn sharp left and follow the fence to the corner and bear slightly left away from it to pass a locked gate on your left. Continue uphill through a lovely sessile oak wood on a well marked path. This path meets a fence on your left and a short section of wooden walkway. Easy walking with a protective fence on your right leads to a path junction. Instead of going down the steps to your right continue straight ahead high above the gorge to a bridge over the stream (**Pont 4 – Pont Uchaf**). There is a fine picnic site here complete with tables, benches and shelter!

'Cross to the clearing over the narrow gorge
Reach a meadow above the falls
the sound of quiet whispers
Rest, watch and listen to the murmur,
the tales of the stream
Mysterious Dolgoch'

2 Return to the steps that descend steeply – now on your left. Go down these and follow the zig-zag path down to stream level. There are good views of the upper falls from this path. Two adits are seen to your left – the last just before the bridge with two names. Pont yr Ogof is one and Pont y Bwa which I think is far more apt – the curved bridge. This is **Pont 3**.

'Pass the cave, dangling over a cauldron –
a blue basin rock clinging to the cliff.
Dangling iron hanging over a precipice
oak and steel over water'

Keep following the path with the stream to your left past another picnic area. Another adit is passed with two shelters beyond to your right. Continue to the fenced-off shaft and bridge over the top of the lower falls. This is **Pont 2** – Pont y Pistyll Arian.

'Footbridge over falls
gurgling along the green grey rocks
sliding, zigzagging
See the white fountain – a silver riband
swallowed by a whale of water roaring
falls'

Cross the bridge, go up steps and continue ahead passing a 'no entry' sign on your left and descend a zig-zag path down to stream level by the lower falls where there is a great view of these. Follow the level path downstream to **Pont 1** – Pont Mur Mwswgl.

'Amber iron flowing from the green moss
Damp gorge split by smooth water
The woodland welcomes
under the large arched viaduct
Follow the track ahead'

Cross the bridge and retrace your steps back to the car park.

Dolgoch Falls were bequeathed to the public through the generosity of a Tywyn chemist – R. J. Roberts – at the turn of the 20th century. Many improvements were made to the area in 2003 by the Bryncrug Community Council with help from the Snowdonia National Park Authority. The viaduct you walk underneath near the start that carries the Talyllyn Railway was built at a cost of £3000 in 1866.

The gorge is a veritable fern garden. The damp atmosphere from the spray of the waterfalls ensures that there are many varieties perfectly at home here including the scarce Wilson's filmy fern. There are also ten species of liverwort which in times past were believed to cure people of liver disease!

evel

픽 picnic

old level

old level

Upper Falls

picnic 픽

②

Dolgoch Falls

19

THE TARRENS & THE PILGRIMS' WAY

DESCRIPTION This is a fine and very diverse walk. Beautiful woodland and stream at the start followed by a forestry track leads to a steep ascent onto the Tarren ridge. This is remote and unspoilt by crowds. Wonderful mountain scenery followed by a descent into history to remind us of how life was all those years ago. 9 miles, 6½ hours.

START The Post Office/Community Centre/Café car park in the middle of Abergynolwyn.

DIRECTIONS From Tywyn take the A493 Dolgellau road as far as Bryncrug. Turn right here on to the B4405 signed Talyllyn. At Abergynolwyn turn right opposite the Railway Inn into the car park.

From the car park walk towards Nant Gwernol station on the Tal-y-llyn railway. Go steeply up the tarmac road to turn right off the road signed for the station. Follow this path through the wood above a lovely clear stream. At a path junction go left up the slope and continue just above the stream – *spot your pool for a chilly swim on the return* – to another junction. Go right over the footbridge to the station. Just before the station there is a post with different coloured path marks. Go left here and initially follow the yellow marks. Go up to the level part and look for yellow and purple marks on your left. At the path junction turn sharp left. Continue to an old winding house called Alltwylt. Follow the line of the old railway. At a footbridge on your left bear right (remains of old incline) and follow blue and purple marker poles. Walk up the right hand side of Nant Moelfre, past some zig-zags and on to a footbridge on the left. Do not cross this but walk ahead (blue marker pole). Keep on this path to a forestry track.

2 Turn left here up the track. Ignore the left turning and keep going gradually uphill.

Go past an obvious right hand turn. Keep going to the next right-hand turn – there is a small pond opposite this turning. Do not turn but go straight ahead and the track bears left to a pull-in for forest vehicles on the left. Up to your right you will notice a notch in the skyline. There is a path, albeit faint, up to this notch over an obvious, shaley, slope that turns into a gully near the top and emerges on the ridge at the right end of some sheep pens. Follow the fence line with the fence to your right to a stile. Go over and continue up the ridge with the fence on your left. Step over the fence by the summit of Tarrenhendre – 634m – and over stile to the summit cairn – a small pile of stones on a peat hag!

3 Return over the stile and continue with the fence on your left towards a prominent ancient cairn. Go over the stile and start going downhill with the fence on your left. *Great views of Cadair Idris and the Afon Dyfi.* Keep going downhill to a stile. Go over this and continue down, still following the fence. Pass a stile on your left and continue gradually uphill to summit. Continue along the narrower ridge to a ladder stile. Follow the path on the far side initially between fences. Keep ahead when the right hand path turns off right. Keep going for a considerable distance to a stile. Go over this and continue along the path through a young plantation. This path bears left to go over a stile at a col, followed by two others. Go over the right of the two if ascending Tarren y Gesail. If you

Abergynolwyn

START

Nant Gwernol Station

② ①

Tarrenhendre 667 m

S ③

20

have had enough then go over the left hand one.

4 Follow the fence tour right up the steep grassy slope to a cairn on the summit ridge. Go left to a stone trig point and crude shelter – 667m. From here descend south-west to find a track at the corner of the forest just above the stream. Go through the gate and follow the well-marked path above the stream on your left to a stile on the right of a gate. Go over this to the lovely Pont Llaeron.

join with a track coming obliquely from your right. Go straight ahead – note the purple marker pole on your left. Ignore the stile on your left and continue to a rustic kissing gate on your left signed to the station. Go through the gate and descend the steep zig-zag path to where the path almost reaches the stream. Follow the good path to a footbridge. Do not cross over but continue down the true right bank of the stream. *The crystal clear water of the Nant Gwernol is below and the walk through the wood is*

Tarren y Gesail
667 m

Bryn Eglwys
Quarry

0   Miles   ½

Pont
Llaeron

alternative

(If you have decided that enough is enough, go over the left hand of the two stiles at the col and follow the path to reach Pont Llaeron easily, although somewhat prickly at times due to overhanging branches of pines. Rejoin the main route at this point).

5 Return to the path and continue gradually downhill to a stile – this section can be very boggy at times. Go over the stile and gradually descend through workings and a mixed wood to a stile. Go over this and turn right along track. Pass to the left of a huge hole – Bryn Eglwys Quarry – and descend to a gate. Follow a good track beyond to

a delightful end. At the path junction go down left to the footbridge leading across to the station but do not cross it. Continue down the route of your outbound journey back to your car in Abergynolwyn.

*C**adfan's Way or Pilgrims' Way** is the old way from Machynlleth by Bryn Eglwys to Abergynolwyn and Twywyn. It was a sheltered route crossing over at the lowest point of the ridge and was reputed to end at the holy island of Bardsey.*

*M**ountain farmers** in the 18th and 19th centuries practised 'transhumance'. They and their families would move to their mountain home – HAFOD – in the summer along with all their animals and return to their valley home – HENDRE – in the autumn.*

NANT GWERNOL FOREST & BRYN EGLWYS QUARRY

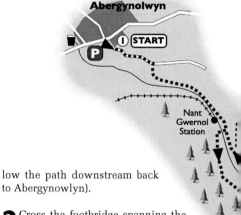

Abergynolwyn

DESCRIPTION Beautiful woodland and a stream followed by wandering through old quarry remains with a return through the woodland. 4 miles, allow 2¾ hours (**alternative 1** is 2 miles, allow 1½ hours; **alternative 2** is 3 miles, allow 2 hours).

START The Post Office/Community Centre/Café car park in the middle of Abergynolwyn.

DIRECTIONS From Tywyn take the A493 Dolgellau road as far as Bryncrug. Turn right here on to the B4405 signed Talyllyn. At Abergynolwyn turn right opposite the Railway Inn into the car park.

I From the car park walk towards Nant Gwernol station on the Tal-y-llyn railway. Go steeply up the tarmac road to turn right off the road signed for the station. Follow this path through the wood above a lovely clear stream. At a path junction go left up slope and continue just above the stream – spot your pool for a swim on the return – to another junction. Go right over footbridge to the station. Just before the station there is a post with different colour path marks. Turn left here. Go up to where the path bears left and follow this (wood fence on your left). A couple of zigzags cross the incline. The path continues to a marker post with coloured arrows. Turn sharply to your left here and continue to the old Alltwylt winding house at the top of the incline where there are the remains of the old railway lines. The path is now level as it follows the line of the old tramway. By a footbridge down to your left bear right (with the remains of the Cantrybedd incline ahead) and follow the path round and up the right hand side of Nant Moelfre, past some zigzags and on to a footbridge on the left. (**Alternative 1** crosses the footbridge down to your left just before you bear right at the old Cantrybedd incline. Turn left after crossing the bridge and fol-

low the path downstream back to Abergynolwyn).

2 Cross the footbridge spanning the Nant Moelfre and follow the path up and past the remains of the Cantrybedd cottages to join a forest road. Turn left. A few metres further there is a track junction. Follow the higher right hand of the two tracks and continue until you reach a Monkey Puzzle tree on your right. Just before the tree turn right up the remains of the old Cwmcwm incline to the ruins of a drum house at the top. Walk left along the level track until a no entry sign is reached. Bear left and follow the path down through spoil heaps to an information board relating to the Narrow Vein. Continue on down the Boundary incline to rejoin the main track 150 metres beyond the monkey puzzle tree. (Instead of going up the Cwmcwm incline **alternative 2** follows the track around from the monkey puzzle tree to this point).

3 Turn right and walk past a marker post on your right and continue along the track passing the site of the Old Mill on your right. Continue along the track bearing left past the ruins of the Manager's House and the New Mill. Keep on the track until you reach a stile to the left of a gate. Cross this and continue past a huge hole on your right – Bryn Eglwys Quarry – and descend to a gate. Go through this and follow a good track beyond to join up with a track coming obliquely from your right. Continue straight ahead. Ignore the stile and gate on your left and continue to a rustic kissing gate on your left. A sign here

22

indicates the way to the station. Go through the gate and descend the steep zigzag path to where the path almost reaches the stream. Follow the good path to a footbridge. Do not cross over but continue down the true right bank of the stream. The water of the Nant Gwernol below is crystal clear and the walk through the wood is a delightful end to the walk. At the path junction 90 down left to the footbridge leading across to the station but do not cross. Continue down the route of your outbound journey back to your car in Abergynolwyn.

Bryn Eglwys Quarry

There are no houses in the Nant Gwernol valley today. At one time there were about 300 men quarrying slate for the huge increase in demand for roofing slates and at its peak in 1877 some 8,000 tons of slate was produced. John Pugh of Penegoes, a village near Machynlleth, opened up the quarry at Bryn Eglwys in 1844. In 1864 it was taken over by the Aberdyfi Slate Company Ltd who built 70 houses in Abergynolwyn.

The cost of producing slate was high and the company unprofitable so the quarry was sold in 1881 to William McConell whose family ran it until it was sold again in 1911 to Mr (who later became Sir) Henry Haydn Jones MP. The quarry closed in 1946.

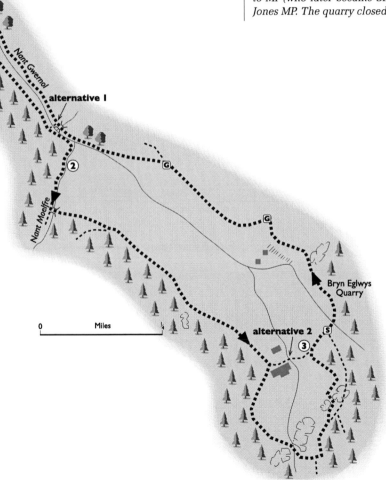

TALYLLYN VIEWS

DESCRIPTION This walk follows the road from Minffordd towards Talyllyn as far as the deserted Pentre Farm. A waymarked path leads through a wood to cross a stream with some pretty cascades to reach open country. From a high point at Rhiwogof the path descends and enters another wood to reach Pen-y-bont Hotel before following the road back to the car park. (This walk can be shortened by starting at Pen-y-bont Hotel and returning there. There is a car parking charge of £5 or a receipt from the bar!) 4½ miles, 2½ hours, or, if doing the shortened version 2½ miles, 1½ hours.

START The car park at Minffordd as for the Minffordd path up Cadair Idris.

DIRECTIONS From Twywn take the A493 Dolgellau road as far as Bryncrug. Turn right here on to the B4405 signed Talyllyn and follow the road through Abergynolwyn. Drive past Talyllyn and just before joining the A487 turn left into the Minffordd car park.

1 From the car park walk towards and past the toilet block to where there is a gate. Go through this gate to join a track. Cross over this on to a well made gravel path. Follow this path to another gate. Go through this and pass through a kissing gate to join the B4405. Walk down the road. Where the road turns sharp left there is a gate in front of you. Go through this onto a very narrow tarmac road. Follow this to a ford. This is avoided by crossing the footbridge on your right. Carry on down the road passing through three gates. After the third gate go up to your right to another gate – with a waymark.

2 Go through this gate and follow the grassy track half-left towards the near-derelict house of Pentre Farm. Just before the house there is a waymark on a fence post. Keep to the right of this and follow the path, with the fence to your left, to a gate. Go through the gate and cross a footbridge just beyond. Walk uphill to a gate. Go through this gate and turn right as indicated by the waymark, walking up the field passing a

waymark and up to another. Turn left here to join a track. Keep on this track – *good views of Talyllyn* – as it slants across the field. When the track levels keep the fence on your left and continue easily to a gate with a waymark. Go through this to Rhiwogof, keeping the fence/hedge on your right. Do not enter the farm area but go left just before the farm to a ladder stile. Cross this and join a good track coming from the farm.

3 Walk down this track to a cattle grid. Immediately after this there is a waymarked path on your left. This path slants rightwards down the hill through the wood until an obvious track is reached coming up from your left. Turn sharp left down this to join a bridleway which continues to the narrow tarmac road. Turn left along this road to a gate before the road drops slightly to the shore of the lake. Keep following the road to a gate just before Pentre Farm. Go through this to return to your car.

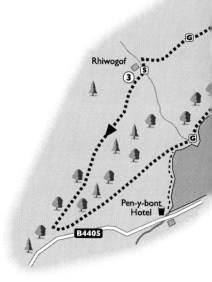

To do the shortened walk, start from the Pen-y-bont Hotel. This makes a good excursion for an evening. Follow the narrow tarmac road to Pentre Farm going through two gates. At the third gate (do not go through)there is a gate up to your left with a waymark. Follow directions **2** and **3** above. When the bridleway joins the narrow tarmac road turn right back to Pen-y-bont.

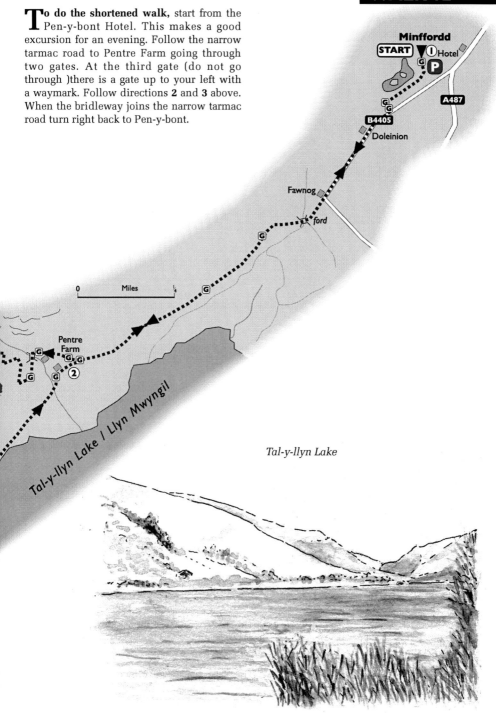

Tal-y-llyn Lake

25

HAPPY VALLEY PANORAMA

DESCRIPTION This pastoral walk travels through much farmland and some lovely woods. There are some very fine views on the walk, inland along the length of Cwm Maethlon and out to sea along the coast of Cardigan Bay. 5 miles, 2½ hours.

START At Cwm Maethlon Chapel.

DIRECTIONS From Tywyn take the A493 road towards Aberdyfi road as far as the Toll House where a sign on the left indicates Cwm Maethlon and Happy Valley. Turn left here and follow this minor road to the Chapel where there is room for two or three cars. Please park safely and considerately as the road is narrow.

I Walk back down the road to a white gate on your left indicating that the road leads to Gwyddgwion. Go through the gate and walk up the narrow road to the top of the rise. There is a gate straight ahead with a waymark sign. Low down there is an old metal sign indicating the Panorama Walk and Aberdyfi. Go through the gate and follow the path keeping the fence to your left. Pass a rocky knoll to your right still keeping the fence to your left and enter a fine avenue of hazel trees. This leads to a ladder stile. Go over this and following an improving path eventually turning into a track as a stream is reached. Follow the track between hedges to a pond just before Dyffryn-glyn-cul. At the end of the pond turn left, go through a gate and on to a ladder stile.

2 Go over this and walk steeply up the field keeping the fence to your left to a track. Cross over this to a ladder stile, to the right of a gate. Climb over the stile and turn sharp right up the grassy continuation of the track heading seaward to a stile. Go over this and on to a waymark. Follow the direction indicated as the track disappears here, *with superb views here both inland and seaward.* Carry on in the same direction and you will soon encounter a lone waymark pole

in the middle of the field. Turn left here as indicated and on to another waymark sited among some quartz boulders. Keep going straight and a faint track develops. Carry on to a waymark. Go down to a gate with a stile to its left. Go over the stile and turn left and follow the fence line to a waymark by a gate. Go through the gate and keep close to the fence on your left past a waymark and on to a gate. Go through the gate on to a narrow tarmac road. Turn right and follow the road. At a track/road junction follow the track straight ahead to keep the covered reservoir on your right. Continue and pass through a gate – *there is a great view of Borth Bog here.* At the track junction by the white cottage go straight ahead to join a narrow tarmac road. Turn left. Ignore the right turn to Llyn Barfog and walk up to the chalet park. Cross the cattle grid and then bear left to join a rough track. Do not walk through the chalets.

Dyffryn-glyn-cul

Ffridd Cefn-isaf

3 Turn right at the track and walk up to and through a gate. Keep going on the rough track. Just after it levels out go over a stile to the left of two gates and walk across a field close to the fence on your right. Go through a gate – *enjoy the superb views of Happy Valley and Corlan Fraith.* Walk half-right steeply downhill across the field to a ladder stile. Go over this and keeping the fence to your left continue to a junction with a track coming from your right. Bear left along the track which doubles as a stream at times! Keep going to a waymark and a much more well-defined track. Turn left along this and descend steeply to a gate. Go through the gate and continue to another which is passed to reach the Afon Dyffryn-gwyn. Fortunately

26

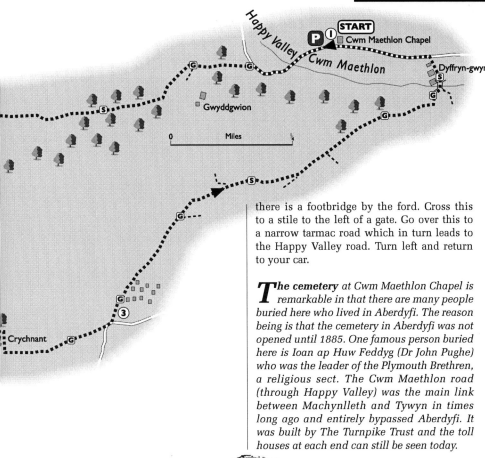

there is a footbridge by the ford. Cross this to a stile to the left of a gate. Go over this to a narrow tarmac road which in turn leads to the Happy Valley road. Turn left and return to your car.

The cemetery at Cwm Maethlon Chapel is remarkable in that there are many people buried here who lived in Aberdyfi. The reason being is that the cemetery in Aberdyfi was not opened until 1885. One famous person buried here is Ioan ap Huw Feddyg (Dr John Pughe) who was the leader of the Plymouth Brethren, a religious sect. The Cwm Maethlon road (through Happy Valley) was the main link between Machynlleth and Tywyn in times long ago and entirely bypassed Aberdyfi. It was built by The Turnpike Trust and the toll houses at each end can still be seen today.

Happy Valley

27

WALK 14
CWM MAETHLON CIRCULAR

DESCRIPTION Wilderness, farmland and extensive views, this walk has it all. From the serenity of Cwm Maethlon you enter the wild and barren hills high above the valley before crossing over the head of it and on to the tranquil Llyn Barfog or Bearded Lake.

START At the Llyn Barfog car park in Cwm Maethlon. 8 miles, 5 hours. ((9½ miles, 5½ hours if the ascent of Corlan Fraith is included).

DIRECTIONS From Tywyn take the A493 road towards Aberdyfi as far as the Toll House where a sign on the left indicates Cwm Maethlon and Happy Valley. Turn left here and follow this minor road to the Snowdonia National Park car park for Llyn Barfog.

I From the car park turn left down the road you have just driven along, go past the turning into Bryndinas and continue to a waymarked path on your right at a sign to Erw Faethlon. Walk through the gate and follow the track. At the track junction before the farm turn right at the waymark and go through a gate and another immediately after. Follow the green path uphill until a gate and ladder stile to right is reached. The large cairn on top of Corlan Fraith is well seen from here. Continue on the wide, green track. Where the path levels there is a gate and ladder stile on right. Go over the ladder stile and continue to the finger post seen ahead. Follow the right hand track if you do not want to climb Corlan Fraith. Continue along this track until it levels and walk past the track on your left coming across from the Corlan Fraith diversion to a gate and ladder stile. (If climbing Corlan Fraith go left at the finger post and continue along the track until a ramshackle gate is seen on the left. Go through this and go half left to corner of fence which is then followed to the summit for superb views. Retrace your steps and return to the ramshackle gate. Go back through and walk half-left to join the track from the finger post at the gate and ladder stile).

2 Go over the ladder stile and continue to a major junction. The track joining from the left comes up from Rhyd-yr-onen. Turn right along this track and keep walking along it ignoring a track on your right just as Llyn Barfog – across Cwm Maethlon – comes into view. Keep going and on through a gate by a stream. 100m before the next gate look up to your left to where a stone circle will be seen and is worth a visit. Return to the track and continue through a gate and start to descend – *with great views of the Dyfi Valley at this point.* Keep on going down through a gate and another at Pant-yr-on which leads to the road. Turn right up the hill a short distance to a gate and waymark on the left.

3 Turn left through the gate and head downhill to a fence. Follow the fence/wall on your left to a gate at the wall corner. Go through this and turn left to follow a drainage ditch to a marker post. Continue down to a stile to the left of a gate. Go over this then go half-right to a ladder stile. Cross this then follow the fence up to your left to a gate. Go right here across a field to an upright stone opposite the fence corner. Go through the gate on your left onto a farm track.

4 Turn right and just before the farm buildings go down left with the fence on your right to join another farm track at a waymark. Go right across a stone slab bridge and on to a gate. Go through this and the ensuing wood to another gate on the main track and continue along this until it starts to rise gently to a gate. Just beyond this the track rises steeply but soon eases. Continue along and through another gate with a ladder stile on the right. *There are great views of the Dyfi Estuary to your left.* The track rises gently and on through a gate – with a view of Corlan Fraith to the right. Further on at the apex of a long left hand loop of track a grassy path leads off right to Llyn Barfog and Echo Rock.

5 After visiting the lake and Echo Rock return to the track and continue along the 'Panorama Walk' gently rising past Carn March Arthur. Continue past this to the next gate and ladder stile after which the track

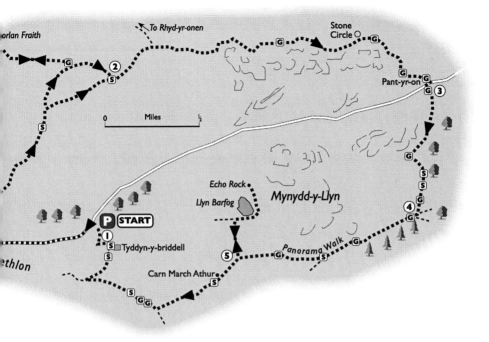

starts to descend to reach the solitary farm house of Bwlch. Go through two gates on to a road and immediately bear half left across the field to a prominent stile over a fence. Go steeply downhill bearing left to a fence corner where there are waymarks. Do not go through the gate here but go half-right down to the next fence where there is a stile. Cross this and go right across the field to cross a small stream and on to a ladder stile. Cross this to join the wide track. Turn left and follow the track back to the car park.

*T*he **Stone Circle** is a prehistoric monument and is called *Eglwys y Gwyddelod.* In John R. Hoyle's book 'A survey of some of the Stone Rings of Mid Wales' he states that it is probable that the ring had eight stones, but no traces can be seen in the surface of the positions of the other two. In the early part of the twentieth century the ring was used for cock fighting with the result that it may have been disturbed.

*L*lyn **Barfog** is in a beautifully isolated situation, its surface covered in water-lilies from late June until September. This may have given it its name, although those more romantically inclined would rather it were named in honour of one of King Arthur's knights – in particular 'the bearded one'. Barfog may have even been Arthur's foster father. There is also, not surprisingly, a fairy-tale associated with the lake, concerning a magical cow which came into the possession of a farmer of Dysyrnant, half-a-mile to the north. This beast gave birth to many fine calves, and provided many gallons of creamy milk. The farmer, as a consequence, became rich. But eventually the cow grew too old, and the farmer decided to employ a butcher to slaughter her. But as the butcher was about to kill the cow, the knife fell from his hand. A little green fairy woman appeared from by the lake, and called the cow, and her calves, home. The fairy and the cows then disappeared into the lake. From then on the farmer's luck changed for the worse.

WALK 15
ANCIENT PATHS

DESCRIPTION Gentle rises, farmland, ancient paths, riverside and superb views all of which makes this a lovely walk – great for an evening. 3 miles, 1½ hours.

START Close to Pont Dysynni on the A493 Tywyn to Dolgellau road.

DIRECTIONS From Tywyn take the A493 Dolgellau road through Bryncrug and continue to Pont Dysynni. There is parking just beyond the bridge on the right hand side of the road or down the second turning after the bridge on your left. Please park carefully on the narrow road.

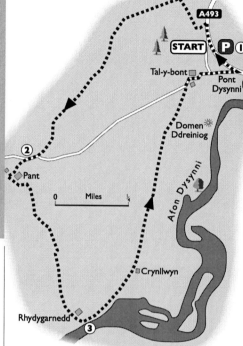

I From the bridge walk along the road in the Dolgellau direction for 300m (100m from the second turning if parked there) to a bridleway sign on your left. Turn left up this and walk up to and through a gate. Go half-right up and across the field on a grassy path to a stile. Go over this and continue half-left across the field passing a small group of boulders before reaching a low col. Here there is an old gate post and a waymark. Ignore the right hand path. Go straight ahead alongside the remains of a ditch on your right. Continue to a gate and go through onto a raised section of track – the remnants of an old road? Walk along this to a gateway (no gate). Go down gradually, still on the old track, and go below a small plantation. Walk on to the next gateway and follow the track gradually down – *there are superb views of Tywyn and Broadwater* – to a gate. Go through this to join a narrow tarmac road. Turn right and shortly reach Pant where there is a marker stone dated 1885.

2 Go past the house and walk to the last of the buildings and go through a gate. Turn sharp left and go over a stile. Go down and around a new farm building on your left and at the end of it walk slightly up the field to a gate. Go through this and on your right almost immediately is a smaller gate. Go through this and walk across the field with the fence on your right to a ladder stile.

Climb over this and keep to the edge of the field with a wall on your right, and continue to a gate with another immediately beyond. Go through both of these and walk across the field close to the wall/hedge on your left to two gates. Go through the right hand one and continue with the fence/wall/hedge on your left to Rhydygarnedd where there is a gate on your left. Pass through this and turn right through the farmyard to another gate. Go through this to reach a tarmac road. Walk through the double gates ahead to reach the Afon Dysynni.

3 Follow the tarmac road, turning right at the two 'T' junctions, back to your car. On your right as you approach Tal-y-bont there is a Motte. *This is called Domen Ddreiniog. There was at one time a ferry that connected Tywyn with Rhydygarnedd. Domen Ddreiniog (thorny mound) was in its day a small fort defending the ford or ferry crossing. Many battles were fought defending river crossings.*

WALK 16

NANT BRAICH-Y-RHIW CIRCULAR

DESCRIPTION A gentle stroll – great for an evening – up the Nant Braich-y-rhiw where there are some good picnic places. The return walk is down a very quiet, leafy lane. 2 miles, 1½ hours

START By the railway bridge close to Rhyd-yr-onen station.

DIRECTIONS From Tywyn take the A493 Dolgellau road as far as Bryncrug. Turn right here on to the B4405 signed Talyllyn. Turn right again some 200m further and drive along the narrow road leading to Rhyd-yr-onen. Parking near the station is very limited. PLEASE park sensibly and DO NOT block any gateways.

I Walk over the railway bridge and up through a gate which has a 'Llwybr Cyhoeddus' (public footpath) sign next to it. Walk up the road to where the tarmac ends and becomes a track. This splits, so go along the left hand track and on through a gate and up to Braich-y-rhiw farm. There are two gates before the farm. Go through the right hand one and pass in front of the house to another gate. Go through this and turn left to go up to and through another gate to the left of a ruin. Walk up the rough track a short distance to where it splits. Go left along the lower track. Continue to a gate by some pines. Nant Braich-y-rhiw is below and to the left of you. Keep on the track and pass to the right of a larch wood to a sheepfold and a gate to the right of it. Go through the gate and continue alongside the stream a short distance before crossing over on a narrow concrete footbridge. A path continues and reaches a road.

2 Turn left and walk down a short way to go through a gate. Continue down the road back to the village.

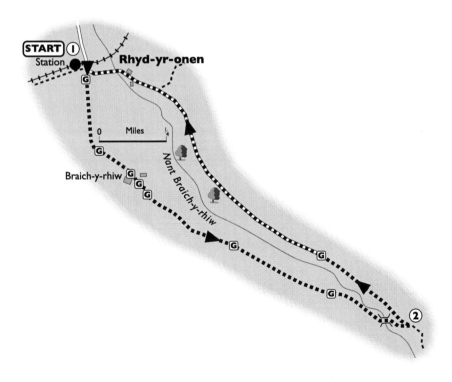

SYLVAN DYSYNNI

DESCRIPTION This is a completely level walk with good riverside and valley views. Ynysmaengwyn wood is well worth exploring before returning to Tywyn and the interesting St. Cadfan's Church. 5 miles, 2½ hours.
START At St. Cadfan's Church in Tywyn.
DIRECTIONS It is possible to park cars behind St Cadfan's Church in Tywyn.

I From your car walk back to the main road and right along the main street passing firstly the Market Hall on your right and subsequently the Tourist Information centre on your left. Keep walking along the street until you turn right down Idris Villas. This is by the sharp bend on the A493. Continuing ahead leads onto the beach. Walk down Idris Villas ignoring all turnings until you come to a level crossing. Just before this turn right and walk parallel to the railway line until past all the houses on your right. Just before the de-restriction signs turn right – waymark – and walk along the rough road to a gate. Go through this and turn left along a rough tarmac track. Continue along this track straight ahead until it ends at a flag pole where there are waymarks. Turn left then immediately right to walk over a foot-bridge. There are stiles at each end, *and good views of the Beacon and the Dysynni Valley.*

2 Go half right to join a path that follows the edge of Broadwater. *Birdlife abounds here.* Follow this path until a low dam can be crossed to a gate. There are steps on the gate to climb over! Bear left along the embankment/dam. Ignore a right turn and keep going along this raised section. Rhydygarnedd is

seen on the opposite bank and the remains of the old jetty. Continue to a stile. Go over this and turn right to go over a concrete foot-bridge. You are now in Ynysmaengwyn Wood containing the ruins of Ynysmaengwyn. *This is a great place to explore on your own, with some quite exotic trees and many flowers in summer.* Having explored return to the foot-bridge and stile.

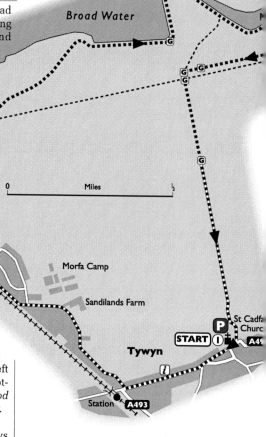

3 Retrace your steps a few metres and go down a path on your left to join a drainage ditch. The path is followed with ditch to your left to a gate. Go through this and on to a waymark. Walk left to go over a footbridge after going through another two gates. Go straight ahead, ignoring the right hand path, along the well defined track to a gate. Go through this and quickly reach a tarmac continuation that takes you to the car park behind St. Cadfan's Church.

Ynysmaengwyn has a history stretching as far back as 1217. Maurice Fitzgerald an Irishman came over to help Llywelyn Fawr (who had built Castell y Bere some years earlier. He was rewarded with a heiress. Several heiresses later one married a Roger Corbet – a Royalist in the Civil War. In 1635 the mansion was burnt to the ground by the Royalists to avoid the Roundheads gaining control. After it was replaced, a grand rebuilding commenced in 1758. A dovecote housed over 800 birds. In the late 1880s the gardens were said to be the finest in the principality with rare trees. Belgian refugees were housed here during the First World War but during the Second World War upkeep was impossible and it was requisitioned as a Royal Marines' Camp. After the war it was given to Merioneth County Council who then gave it to Tywyn County Council in 1948. The end came when Ynysmaengwyn was fired as an exercise for the Fire Service and the ruins razed by the army! A full account can be obtained from the Tourist Information Centre in Tywyn.

The Broad Water

THE OLD POSTMAN'S WALK

DESCRIPTION This walk follows an old post route from Rhyd-y-criw to Blaidd. There are good views, woodland and a lovely stream. Towards the end of the walk the church of Saint Mary and Saint Egryn is well worth looking in. 2½ miles, 1½ hours.

START The village hall – Neuadd Egryn – in Llanegryn.

DIRECTIONS From Tywyn take the A493 Dolgellau road and drive through Bryncrug. Continue across Pont Dysynni to a right turn signed Llanegryn. Turn right here and drive into the village. Just before the bridge over the stream and a left turn, turn down to your right where the village hall – Neuadd Egryn – is prominently marked. There is ample parking here.

1 Walk back to the road and go over the bridge. Turn left, following the direction indicated to the school and church. Immediately after the last building turn left through a gate with a Llwybr Cyhoeddus (Public footpath) sign. Follow the grassy meadow past a play area and continue to a kissing gate. Go through this to join a tarmac road. Turn left. A few metres further on turn right to go over a ladder stile. Turn right where the path appears to split, to join and follow a stream on your right. The path is narrow but very well marked and goes up a small wooded valley with the occasional step to a level area. *There are good views of the church of Saint Mary and Saint Egryn here.* Continue to a stile. Go over this and ignore the footbridge on your right. Go left opposite the bridge onto a less well marked path and walk away from the stream up to a ladder stile.

2 Go over this and walk across the field veering slightly right to pass to the right of a large group of boulders to the corner of the field and the coppice. Go through the gate and walk across another field to a wooden gate where there is a waymark. There is a boggy section half way across! Go through the gate and go slightly left to a ladder stile which is to the left of two gates. Continue into the farmyard and up to the farmhouse. The old postal route passes in front of the house and into an impenetrable section of path. This is avoided by walking past the house to the left along a track to a gate. Do not go through the gate ahead. Go through the gate on your right and follow the fence on your right to walk above Rhyd-y-criw. Join the fence again on your right and follow this to a gate. Go through this and continue for another 100m to a gate on your left. Pass through this and walk in the same line through a gateway. Ignore the gate on your right but continue to a stile with a waymark. Go over this and walk down through the farmyard to a stile.

3 Climb over this stile into a field. Walk down this, keeping the fence on your left, to a footbridge over a boggy bit, to reach a ladder stile shortly after. Climb over the stile and walk half-left to a go over another ladder stile on a short section of wall. Follow the edge of the field keeping the fence on your left to another ladder stile, right of a gate. Climb over this. Walk down the field with a stream to your left and drop down to a stile and footbridge. Ignore the obvious gate ahead but go across the footbridge and walk down the field with the stream now on your right. Part way down the field head up to a fence on your left and continue to a gate. Go through this and turn left through another. Walk past the farmhouse to join a tarmac road. *The church of Saint Mary and Saint Egryn is now on your right. A visit is highly recommended.* From the church walk along the road to a 'T' junction. Turn right and walk down the hill back into the village and your car, ignoring the right turn.

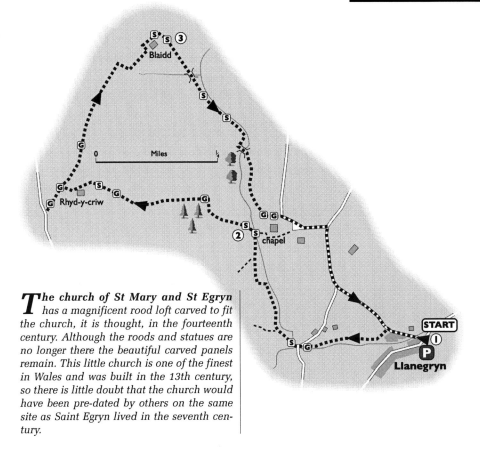

*T*he church of St Mary and St Egryn
has a magnificent rood loft carved to fit
the church, it is thought, in the fourteenth
century. Although the roods and statues are
no longer there the beautiful carved panels
remain. This little church is one of the finest
in Wales and was built in the 13th century,
so there is little doubt that the church would
have been pre-dated by others on the same
site as Saint Egryn lived in the seventh century.

St Mary & St Egryn

AROUND CYNFAL FACH SPUR

DESCRIPTION A very seldom walked area which takes you into the mountains but without the problems associated with higher mountains walking. A lovely start up the Nant Braich-y-rhiw leads to the one very steep section. You then descend to lowland sheep pastures. The final stretch is alongside the Talyllyn Railway. 5 miles, 3½ hours.

START By the railway bridge close to Rhyd-yr-onen station.

DIRECTIONS From Tywyn take the A493 Dolgellau road as far as Bryncrug. Turn right here on to the B4405 signed Talyllyn. Turn right again some 200m further and drive along the narrow road leading to Rhyd-yr-onen. Parking near the station is very limited. PLEASE park sensibly and DO NOT block any gateways.

I Walk over the railway bridge and up through a gate which has a 'Llwybr Cyhoeddus' (public footpath) sign next to it. Walk up the road to where the tarmac ends and becomes a track. This splits, so go along the left hand track and on through a gate and up to Braich-y-rhiw farm. There are two gates before the farm. Go through the right hand one and pass in front of the house to another gate. Go through this and turn left up to, and through, another gate to the left of a ruin. Walk up the rough track a short distance to where it splits. Go left along the lower track. Continue to a gate by some pines. Nant Braich-y-rhiw is below and to the left of you. Keep on the track and pass to the right of a larch wood to a sheepfold and a gate to the right of it. Go through the gate and continue alongside the stream a short distance before crossing over on a footbridge. A path continues and reaches a road. Turn right along this to where the tarmac ends.

2 Walk gradually up along the well defined track until a fence is seen to your right on the opposite side of the stream. Find a suit-

able place to cross – take care in wet weather. There are now no paths until you are well down Cwm Cynfal, with only stiles marking the way! Follow the fence on your left steeply up the hillside until close to the top where it is possible to go diagonally right to join a fence. Walk along this until a stile is found. Go over this and bear right. After a very short ascent, a very gradual descending contour across the hillside leads to a stile in the next fence. Cross the tiny stream before the stile and go over it to cross a field. Keep Nant Cynfal to your right and cross the field to a gate. Go through this and two more gates after which a track is followed. Continue and go through another gate where the track splits. Take the lower right hand one and continue down to a gate. Go through this and keep following the track with a fence to your right. When the fence ends and where there is a stunted rowan tree on your left look for a yellow-topped pole across the field. Go half right over this and go towards the stile. Go half-right across the field to the fence corner where there is a footbridge and stile.

3 Cross these and go half-left up the field to a stile. Go over this – boggy ground just beyond – and follow the path. Go over a stile close to Fach-goch and continue to the last building where a gate on the right is passed. This leads onto a waymarked track. Follow the track through a gate and keep on this track until it joins the Talyllyn Railway. Do not walk on the lines but follow a path with a fence to your left. Go through three gates. After passing through the third one a tarmac road is joined. Go straight across this and through a waymarked gate. Continue alongside the railway to a stile to the right of a gate. Climb over this and on to a ladder stile which is crossed to join the road. Turn left and go over the bridge back to your car.

36

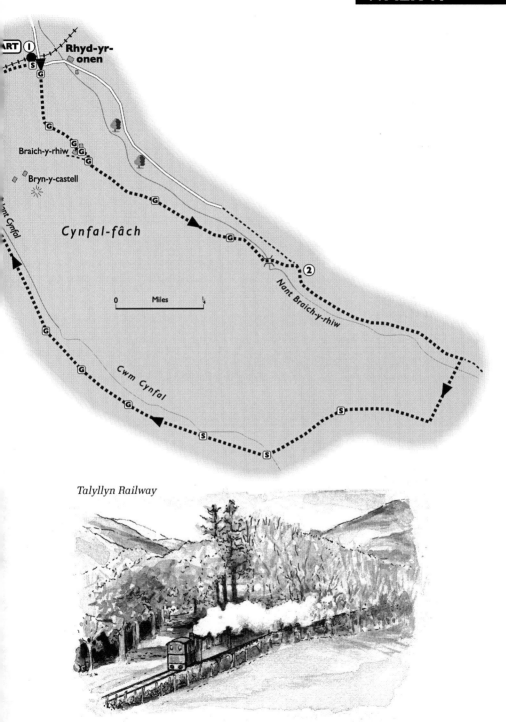

Talyllyn Railway

THE BEACON ROUND

DESCRIPTION Apart from being on a high mountain top, the Beacon must have the best views of anywhere, especially as it only as it is only 178m high. It is possible to see all the way down the Cardigan Bay coastline, Snowdon, Lleyn peninsula, the Dysynni Valley with Birds' Rock almost as dominant as Cadair Idris. With only one steep uphill section the remainder of the walk is along grassy paths or bridleways across farmland or through small wooded areas. **START** At the large pull-in on the left-hand side of the road 200 metres before Tonfannau station. 5½ miles, 3¼ hours.

DIRECTIONS From Tywyn take the A493 Dolgellau road through Bryncrug and continue to Pont Dysynni. Immediately beyond the bridge turn left and drive along this very narrow road to Llechlwyd. Continue along the road passing some large and very substantial quarry gates on your right, with a large warning sign attached. 600 yards further on there is a large pull-in on your left, where cars may be parked.

1 Walk back past the quarry gates and through the tiny village of Llechlwyd to a bridleway sign on your left after ¾ mile. You are now on the eastern side of the Beacon. Turn left up the bridleway and go through a gate. Continue along the gradually rising rough track across the base of the hill to a gate. Do not go through this but climb steeply up the hill passing a water tank on your right to a well marked path and walk through a gateway to where the gradient eases. Then go half-right up the hill to a ladder stile over the wall above. Before going over the stile walk left below the wall to the second gap. Go through this and on to the summit where there are the remains of the old beacon and a trig point.

2 Retrace your steps to the stile and go over it. Walk half-right up the slope at first then go down to a ladder stile. Go over this and walk half right again down to a gate. Go through this and head straight across open land going gently down to where walls on each side of you converge and there are two gates. Go through the right hand one and follow the green track down to a gate. Pass through the gate and bear left to another gate where there is a waymark. Turn right in front of a house, bear left and continue on to join a tarmac road.

3 Turn left down this road. Ignore the left turn just before a house, Castell y Delyn. Just before the next house on the left, Bryntirion, there is a partly hidden waymark.

Turn left and go up a leafy section through three gates. After going through the third gate cross the field with the wall to your right to a kissing gate. Continue across the field to a waymarked stile which is climbed over into another field. Keep close to the wall/fence on your right. When the wall ends at a waymark drop down the slope to a fence above a house. Keep following this waymarked wall/fence line to where the gorse bushes end. Here go half-left across the field (there is a large boulder on the grassy path part way along) to a gate at the corner of the field just before a house. Go through the gate onto a tarmac road at a public footpath sign.

4 Turn left and walk down the road to a bridleway sign on your left again just before a house. Turn left up this grassy path to a gate. Go through this and follow the green track to a gate at Tyddyn Meurig. Pass through the gate to a track and bear left up to another gate on the right. Continue through the gate and ignore the gate on the right. Follow the track with a wall on your right and continue through a gateway and on to a gate. Go through this and walk behind Bronclydwr. Continue through the wood, where the path is overgrown in places, into the open again and on to a gate. Go through this and on to another just before some pine trees. Pass through this and almost immediately go over

Tonfanau Station

STAR
P

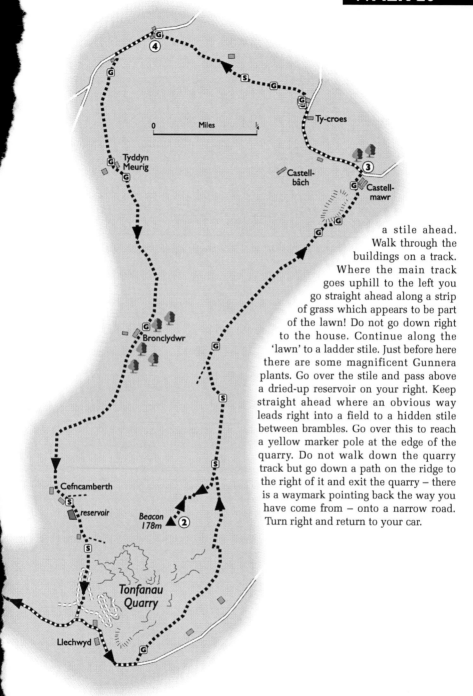

0   Miles   ½

Ty-croes

Tyddyn
Meurig

Castell-
bâch

Castell-
mawr

Bronclydwr

Cefncamberth

reservoir

Beacon
178m

Tonfanau
Quarry

Llechwyd

a stile ahead. Walk through the buildings on a track. Where the main track goes uphill to the left you go straight ahead along a strip of grass which appears to be part of the lawn! Do not go down right to the house. Continue along the 'lawn' to a ladder stile. Just before here there are some magnificent Gunnera plants. Go over the stile and pass above a dried-up reservoir on your right. Keep straight ahead where an obvious way leads right into a field to a hidden stile between brambles. Go over this to reach a yellow marker pole at the edge of the quarry. Do not walk down the quarry track but go down a path on the ridge to the right of it and exit the quarry – there is a waymark pointing back the way you have come from – onto a narrow road. Turn right and return to your car.

PRONUNCIATION

These basic points should help non-Welsh speakers

Welsh	English equivalent
c	always hard, as in cat
ch	as on the Scottish word loch
dd	as 'th' in then
f	as 'f' in of
ff	as 'ff' in off
g	always hard as in got
ll	no real equivalent. It is like 'th' in then, but with an 'L' sound added to it, giving 'thlan' for the pronunciation of the Welsh 'Llan'.

In Welsh the accent usually falls on the last-but-one syllable of a word.

KEY TO THE MAPS

- Main road
- Minor road
- Walk route and direction
- (I) Walk instruction
- Path
- River/stream
- G Gate
- S Stile
- △ Summit
- Woods
- Pub
- P Parking

THE COUNTRYSIDE CODE

- Be safe – plan ahead and follow any signs
- Leave gates and property as you find them
- Protect plants and animals, and take your litter home
- Keep dogs under close control
- Consider other people

The CroW Act 2000, implemented throughout Wales in May 2005, introduced new legal rights of access for walkers to designated open country, predominantly mountain, moor, heath or down, plus all registered common land. This access can be subject to restrictions and closure for land management or safety reasons for up to 28 days a year.

Published by
Kittiwake
3 Glantwymyn Village Workshops, Glantwymyn, Machynlleth, Montgomeryshire SY20 8LY

© Text & map research: Des Marshall 2008
© Maps & illustrations: Kittiwake 2008
Drawings by Morag Perrott

Cover photos: *Main* – Looking towards Cadair Idris from the 'true' summit of Birds' Rock, Des Marshall. Inset – Birds' Rock, David Perrott.

Printed by MWL, Pontypool.

ISBN: **978 1902302 64 5**